Men's
ANXIETY DEVOTIONAL WORKBOOK

INCLUDES 31 DAYS OF ACTIVITIES FOR CHRISTIAN MEN TO MANAGE ANXIETY

This workbook addresses Anxiety from a Christian approach

Chanell Finley, M.Ed, LPC-S

Hi there. I'm Chanell Finley and I am a licensed counselor, speaker, author, consultant, and mentor. I am the owner of Chanell Finley & Co. and I believe that every gift I share with the world is thanks to God and my relentless faith as a Christian.

As a speaker, I inspire my audiences to reclaim their voices by taking action and accountability in their lives.

I use my testimony and experiences to influence others who have excelled professionally, but may be facing challenges with self-worth, self-compassion and self-love.

I am also the owner of CF Counseling & Consulting, where I serve adults struggling with anxiety, depression and trauma. I have almost 20 years of experience guiding others towards mental wellness.

I created this workbook as a resource for Christian men who desire to learn and understand effective ways to manage anxiety. My prayer is that God will use this as a tool to help you learn, grow and experience victory in every area of your life.

Chanell Finley

This Workbook Belongs To

_____

TABLE OF CONTENTS

TABLE OF CONTENTS (CONT).

HOW TO USE THIS WORKBOOK

1. **DEVOTIONS AND PRE-ASSESSMENT**
   Complete the preassessment in the intro section and recite each prayer after each devotion with a heart of gratitude and expectancy.

2. **ACTIVITIES & INTERACTIVE EXERCISES**
   Complete all exercises for each chapter to increase self-awareness. Interactive exercises will help to reinforce implementation of coping strategies and faith in scripture.

3. **JOURNAL PROMPTS & NOTES**
   Write your take-aways from each devotion, activity, exercise and note your progress. Express your heart and expect God to meet you where you are.

4. **REFLECTIONS & POST ASSESSMENT**
   Journal your reflections for each chapter, recite your affirmations and complete the post assessment with renewed confidence.

"When we learn how to win the battle in our minds, we will learn just how powerful we are."

Chanell Finley

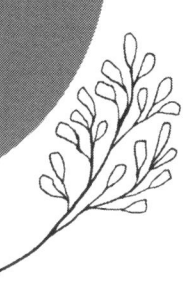

GETTING
STARTED

INTRO

WHAT TO EXPECT FROM THIS WORKBOOK

God's Word is the Final Authority

Introduction

HI THERE! As you begin your journey of healing and taking back your life, I want to say how courageous of you to take this step. It isn't always easy to acknowledge we need help, to then take the step and to seek it. As a believer and more specifically, as a man, the pressures of life may sometimes render you helpless, hopeless and stuck. No matter where you are in your journey, I am excited to help you identify what's hindering you and what'll help you overcome. This workbook was created to help you address anxiety so you can begin living out every dream God has placed inside you.

Anxiety is being discussed more now than ever. Experts and others are beginning to see the totality of its impact on an individual's ability to pivot and maintain daily functioning. For many, things have not been okay for a long time and the horrific effects of the pandemic have exacerbated these emotions and their symptoms.

There's a resounding echo across television, podcasts, and social media of individuals across this world struggling to manage their emotions, struggling to return to life as they once knew it and struggling to maintain the relationships they once deemed significant. So, how do we fix it? How do we believe God's Word and rest in His promises? How do we begin to understand how to move through anxiety to a place called Peace?

Through my own personal experience and in my almost 20 years of mental health experience, I have witnessed the transforming power of emotional healing through God's Word and other resources. Being an overcomer of childhood trauma, there have been times in my adult life where it felt as though I was unable to move through anxiety.

I can remember thinking to myself, "How can I be a Christian and riddled with anxiety? What's wrong with me?" I realized I needed to immerse myself in God's Word and study what it said about my identity in Him. At that time, one of the things I quickly learned was most of my adult life was being lived through a trauma response lens.

I had to make an adjustment to my life's view if I wanted to win the internal battle I was experiencing against anxiety. I had to begin practicing thought and body attunement through somatic work, cognition challenging/reframing, and regulating my central nervous system along with healthier dieting practices.

Remember, as you begin to gain a greater self-awareness, to recognize your gifts and strengths, healing will be on the horizon. Inside this workbook, you will find powerful tools and resources to help you on your journey so you may begin to overcome anxiety. Through step-by-step practices, affirmations, activities, exercises and journal prompts, you'll be motivated to remain steadfast at learning emotional regulation. This workbook is not intended to take the place of therapy, mental health treatment, medication management or seeking needed help from a trained professional. Rather, it is an additional resource to aid in understanding and growth.

I encourage you to take all the time you need to move through this workbook to receive what is necessary to stay the course on your journey. Some exercises may cause apprehension and may feel too vulnerable, but I encourage you to allow your feelings to remain present as you push through to gain greater self-attunement.

I'm excited to be a passenger on your journey, as you are the driver of change. You're a priceless gift to this world and what you have to offer is needed by so many. Thank you for allowing me to take part.

ANXIETY PREASSESSMENT SCREENER

The preassessment below is a self-screener that provides an understanding of your level of anxiety. Please complete it.

Anxiety Screen Questionnaire

GAD-7				
Over the <u>last 2 weeks,</u> how often have you been bothered by the following problems? *(Use "√" to indicate your answer)*	Not at all	Several days	More than half the days	Nearly every day
1. Feeling nervous, anxious or on edge	0	1	2	3
2. Not being able to stop or control worrying	0	1	2	3
3. Worrying too much about different things	0	1	2	3
4. Trouble relaxing	0	1	2	3
5. Being so restless that it is hard to sit still	0	1	2	3
6. Becoming easily annoyed or irritable	0	1	2	3
7. Feeling afraid as if something awful might happen	0	1	2	3

Scoring:

☐ 5 – 9 Mild anxiety

☐ 10 – 14 Moderate anxiety

☐ 15 – 21 Severe anxiety

Total Score T_____ = _____ + _____ + _____

INTENTIONALITY:
LET'S SET SOME GOALS

1. What do I desire to gain from this workbook (understanding, freedom, encouragement, growth, resources, etc).

_____

_____

_____

2. How will I use this workbook in my daily life as a resource (example: "I will set aside 20 mins each morning to read my devotion and complete exercises")?

_____

_____

_____

3. How will I know I am meeting my goals and overcoming anxiety (example: "I do not feel lightheaded anymore when stressed")?

_____

_____

_____

CHAPTER

01

WHEN ANXIETY CHALLENGES YOUR FAITH

Week 1 - God's Word is the Final Authority

When Anxiety Challenges Your Faith
Devotional

Fear is our natural response to stressors, especially those that pose a threat or danger. God created our brain and body to respond this way as a protective factor. However, how we respond to that which creates prolonged, exacerbated anxiety impacts our mental, emotional, physical and spiritual health. God also knew this and addresses anxiety throughout His Word.

Over and over again within the scriptures, we are reminded God is our Comforter. He does not ignore the challenges we endure, and He is not blind to the things we see as threatening to our well-being. Psalm 94:19 reads, "When anxiety was great within me, your consolation brought joy to my soul." God's comfort combats anxiety! When we choose to cast our cares, worries and fear upon Him, we can rest, knowing, the Father is in control. Just as the Father provides consolation, healthy relationships with family, friends and other believers also provide comfort and peace. Look for ways that being connected to family, to friends and to the body of Christ can help you go through your trials encouraged.

Psalm 61:2 reads, "From the end of the earth will I cry unto thee, when my heart is overwhelmed: lead me to the Rock that is higher than I." It's not that there's nothing to worry about – it's that we have to trust the Lord as our King, our Provider, and our Loving Father.

Devotional (cont.)

We have the power to choose to not give into fears and worries over temporary circumstances; but, to instead focus on the victory and eternal promise our Father has for us. Sometimes it has to be a moment-by-moment choice.

In Matthew 6:34, Jesus said, "Therefore do not worry about tomorrow, for tomorrow will worry about itself. Each day has enough trouble of its own." Matthew also states that we aren't gaining anything or adding to our lives if we succumb to worry. As we heed these instructions in Matthew, we must prepare our hearts by seeking Him through His Word. We must live our lives knowing His Word is the FINAL authority.

Worrying about the unknowns of life will zap our energy, tie up our resources and time, and impact our mental, emotional, physical and spiritual health.

Prayer, especially with a focus on gratefulness, is also a vital way to combat anxiety. When we spend time with God, our hearts are focused and resolved to walk with Him. Take a look at the scriptures below.

Philippians 4:6
"Do not be anxious about anything, but in everything by prayer and supplication with thanksgiving let your requests be made known to God."

Devotional (cont.)

Paul gave us clear instructions on combating anxiety with prayer. God wants us to rest in knowing He hears, He sees, He knows, He loves, and He is with us – even when we don't feel it and when we are fighting to stand firm on His Word. He's big enough to hold you and me through all our anxieties.

Psalm 34:7
"When the righteous cry for help, the LORD hears and delivers them out of all their troubles."

The Lord did not design us to live a life of anxiety, but a life that reflects who He is. He is all-powerful, all-knowing, and present everywhere. He made the way through Jesus for you and I to live a life of love, grace, and strength in Him. I Timothy 1:7 notes, "For God gave us a spirit not of fear but of power and love and self-control." Be intentional each day to triumph over anxiety and to live a life of freedom. The Lord is with you.

Prayer

Father,

Thank you for reminding me that I am never alone. Thank you for the reassurance that Your Word is able to comfort me through all my fears. I cast all of my cares upon you because I know and believe you care for me and will do what's necessary to comfort me and give me peace. Lord, I trust you because you've never failed me. Because of your faithfulness, I rest in You. In Jesus' name, Amen.

www.chanellfinley.com

When Anxiety Challenges Your Faith

Instructions: Take a moment to answer the questions below to identify how anxiety challenges your faith.

What does anxiety look like to you in your life right now?

_____

_____

_____

How long have you struggled with anxiety?

_____

_____

_____

How does anxiety impact your daily life?

_____

_____

_____

List positive and negative ways you have been coping with anxiety?

_____

_____

_____

My Daily Feelings Log
Day 1

FEELINGS LIST
angry
annoyed
anxious
ashamed
awkward
brave
calm
cheerful
chill
confused
discouraged
disgusted
distracted
embarrassed
excited
friendly
guilty
happy
hopeful
jealous
lonely
loved
nervous
offended
scared
thoughtful
tired
uncomfortable
unsure
worried

Choose two words from the list to describe how you feel today. Can't find your emotions there? Feel free to use other words.

I think these feelings are:

○ both positive

○ negative and positive

○ positive and negative

○ both negative

I feel this way because_____

_____

_____

_____

_____

What are 2 positive ways I can maintain or manage my emotions today?

When Anxiety Challenges Your Faith

Instructions: Take a moment to reflect on the devotion and the exercises that followed. Meditate on the scripture below and then journal or jot down notes you feel God is speaking to your heart.

Day 1 - Devotional Journaling

"When anxiety was great within me, your consolation brought joy to my soul." - Psalm 94:19

_____

_____

_____

_____

_____

_____

_____

_____

_____

My Daily Feelings Log
Day 2

FEELINGS LIST

angry
annoyed
anxious
ashamed
awkward
brave
calm
cheerful
chill
confused
discouraged
disgusted
distracted
embarrassed
excited
friendly
guilty
happy
hopeful
jealous
lonely
loved
nervous
offended
scared
thoughtful
tired
uncomfortable
unsure
worried

Choose two words from the list to describe how you feel today. Can't find your emotions there? Feel free to use other words.

I think these feelings are:

○ both positive
○ negative and positive

○ positive and negative
○ both negative

I feel this way because_____

_____

_____

_____

_____

What are 2 positive ways I can maintain or manage my emotions today?

When Anxiety Challenges Your Faith

Instructions: Take a moment to reflect on your emotions today and your day overall. Meditate on the scripture below and then journal or jot down notes you feel God is speaking to your heart.

Day 2 - Reflective Journaling

"From the end of the earth will I cry unto thee, when my heart is overwhelmed: lead me to the Rock that is higher than I."

Psalm 61:2

_____

_____

_____

_____

_____

_____

_____

_____

_____

My Daily Feelings Log
Day 3

FEELINGS LIST

angry
annoyed
anxious
ashamed
awkward
brave
calm
cheerful
chill
confused
discouraged
disgusted
distracted
embarrassed
excited
friendly
guilty
happy
hopeful
jealous
lonely
loved
nervous
offended
scared
thoughtful
tired
uncomfortable
unsure
worried

Choose two words from the list to describe how you feel today. Can't find your emotions there? Feel free to use other words.

I think these feelings are:

○ both positive
○ negative and positive

○ positive and negative
○ both negative

I feel this way because _____

_____

_____

_____

_____

What are 2 positive ways I can maintain or manage my emotions today?

When Anxiety Challenges Your Faith

Instructions: Take a moment to reflect on your emotions today and your day overall. Meditate on the scripture below and then journal or jot down notes you feel God is speaking to your heart.

Day 3 - Reflective Journaling

"Therefore do not worry about tomorrow, for tomorrow will worry about itself. Each day has enough trouble of its own."

Matt. 6:34

_____

_____

_____

_____

_____

_____

_____

_____

_____

My Daily Feelings Log
Day 4

FEELINGS LIST

angry
annoyed
anxious
ashamed
awkward
brave
calm
cheerful
chill
confused
discouraged
disgusted
distracted
embarrassed
excited
friendly
guilty
happy
hopeful
jealous
lonely
loved
nervous
offended
scared
thoughtful
tired
uncomfortable
unsure
worried

Choose two words from the list to describe how you feel today. Can't find your emotions there? Feel free to use other words.

I think these feelings are:

○ both positive

○ negative and positive

○ positive and negative

○ both negative

I feel this way because _____

_____

_____

_____

_____

What are 2 positive ways I can maintain or manage my emotions today?

When Anxiety Challenges Your Faith

Instructions: Take a moment to reflect on your emotions today and your day overall. Meditate on the scripture below and then journal or jot down notes you feel God is speaking to your heart.

Day 4 - Reflective Journaling

"I want you to be free from anxieties." I Cor. 7:32

_____

_____

_____

_____

_____

_____

_____

_____

_____

_____

My Daily Feelings Log
Day 5

FEELINGS LIST

angry
annoyed
anxious
ashamed
awkward
brave
calm
cheerful
chill
confused
discouraged
disgusted
distracted
embarrassed
excited
friendly
guilty
happy
hopeful
jealous
lonely
loved
nervous
offended
scared
thoughtful
tired
uncomfortable
unsure
worried

Choose two words from the list to describe how you feel today. Can't find your emotions there? Feel free to use other words.

I think these feelings are:

○ both positive
○ negative and positive

○ positive and negative
○ both negative

I feel this way because _____

_____

_____

_____

_____

What are 2 positive ways I can maintain or manage my emotions today?

When Anxiety Challenges Your Faith

Instructions: Take a moment to reflect on your emotions today and your day overall. Meditate on the scripture below and then journal or jot down notes you feel God is speaking to your heart.

Day 5 - Reflective Journaling

"And which of you by being anxious can add a single hour to his span of life? If then you are not able to do as small a thing as that, why are you anxious about the rest?"

Luke 12:25-26

_____

_____

_____

_____

_____

_____

_____

_____

_____

My Daily Feelings Log
Day 6

FEELINGS LIST

angry
annoyed
anxious
ashamed
awkward
brave
calm
cheerful
chill
confused
discouraged
disgusted
distracted
embarrassed
excited
friendly
guilty
happy
hopeful
jealous
lonely
loved
nervous
offended
scared
thoughtful
tired
uncomfortable
unsure
worried

Choose two words from the list to describe how you feel today. Can't find your emotions there? Feel free to use other words.

I think these feelings are:

○ both positive
○ negative and positive

○ positive and negative
○ both negative

I feel this way because _____

_____

_____

_____

_____

What are 2 positive ways I can maintain or manage my emotions today?

When Anxiety Challenges Your Faith

Instructions: Take a moment to reflect on your emotions today and your day overall. Meditate on the scripture below and then journal or jot down notes you feel God is speaking to your heart.

Day 6 - Reflective Journaling

"Casting all your anxieties on him, because he cares for you." I Pet. 5:7

_____

_____

_____

_____

_____

_____

_____

_____

_____

My Daily Feelings Log
Day 7

FEELINGS LIST

angry
annoyed
anxious
ashamed
awkward
brave
calm
cheerful
chill
confused
discouraged
disgusted
distracted
embarrassed
excited
friendly
guilty
happy
hopeful
jealous
lonely
loved
nervous
offended
scared
thoughtful
tired
uncomfortable
unsure
worried

Choose two words from the list to describe how you feel today. Can't find your emotions there? Feel free to use other words.

I think these feelings are:

○ both positive

○ negative and positive

○ positive and negative

○ both negative

I feel this way because _____

_____

_____

_____

_____

What are 2 positive ways I can maintain or manage my emotions today?

When Anxiety Challenges Your Faith

Instructions: Take a moment to reflect on your emotions today and your day overall. Meditate on the scripture below and then journal or jot down notes you feel God is speaking to your heart.

Day 7 - Reflective Journaling

"Do not be anxious about anything, but in everything by prayer and supplication with thanksgiving let your requests be made known to God." Phil. 4:6

_____

_____

_____

_____

_____

_____

_____

_____

_____

_____

WEEK 1 SCRIPTURE REFLECTIONS

Instructions: Continue meditating on these scriptures throughout your day and the weeks to come.

"When anxiety was great within me, your consolation brought joy to my soul." **Psalm 94:19**

"From the end of the earth will I cry unto thee, when my heart is overwhelmed: lead me to the Rock that is higher than I." **Psalm 61:2**

"Therefore do not worry about tomorrow, for tomorrow will worry about itself. Each day has enough trouble of its own." **Matt. 6:34**

"I want you to be free from anxieties." **I Cor. 7:32**

"And which of you by being anxious can add a single hour to his span of life? If then you are not able to do as small a thing as that, why are you anxious about the rest?" **Luke 12:25-26**

"Casting all your anxieties on him, because he cares for you." **I Pet. 5:7**

"Do not be anxious about anything, but in everything by prayer and supplication with thanksgiving let your requests be made known to God." **Phil. 4:6**

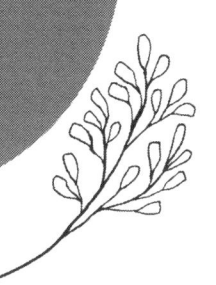

CHAPTER

UNDERSTANDING ANXIETY AND ITS IMPACT

Week 2: God's Word is the Final Authority

UNDERSTANDING ANXIETY - DAY 8

So, what's the difference between fear and anxiety? From our devotion, we learned fear is our natural response to a potential threat or danger. It is a God-given survival instinct intended for our protection. It alerts us to prepare to fight for survival or to run away from impending danger.

Anxiety, on the other hand, is prolonged fear that persists where no real threat ensues - after a threat or danger no longer exists, what appears to be a threat is not, or before there is a potential threat that arises. When left unaddressed, anxiety may become chronic and debilitating, preventing us from being able to function calmly and from experiencing God's peace.

Fear is also referred to as our body's alarm system. With anxiety, the natural response of fear to a perceived threat becomes magnified and is seemingly unable to be turned "off". For clarity, let's take a look at four common stages of anxiety:

1. *Perception of threat/danger* - fear kicks in.
2. *Assessment of threat/danger* - you determine how serious the threat is and if you have the necessary resources to cope.
3. *Psychological and emotional responses* - you feel different physical sensations within the body to deal with the threat/danger and the feeling of fear, itself.
4. *Behavioral response* - You do something to deal with the threat such as facing it, avoiding it, or distracting yourself, etc.

Read it again and process the stages. We will pause here until tomorrow. Be sure to complete today's exercise and journal writing.

On Day 9, we will begin reviewing each stage for greater understanding.

DAILY THOUGHT TRACKER

Identify and process automatic negative thoughts.

Day 8

OCCURRENCE

What happened?

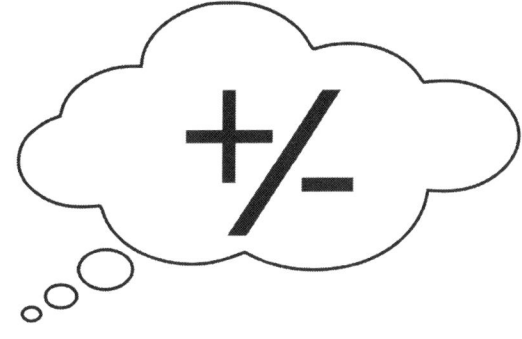

THOUGHTS

How did it make me feel?

EMOTIONS

What thoughts came up when the event was happening?

RESPONSE

What was my response to the situation?

SUPPORTIVE EVIDENCE

Why is my thought true?

NON-SUPPORTIVE EVIDENCE

Why might my thought not be true?

Understanding Anxiety and Its Impact

Instructions: Take a moment to reflect on what you read today and your thoughts today. Meditate on the scripture below and then journal or jot down notes you feel God is speaking to your heart.

Day 8 - Understanding Anxiety

"For God gave us a spirit not of fear but of power and love and self-control." II Tim. 1:7

_____

_____

_____

_____

_____

_____

_____

_____

_____

PERCEPTION OF THREAT/DANGER - DAY 9

For fear to arise, there most often is a threat. This threat may be external, internal or may present as a phobia. I'll briefly provide an explanation of these three types of threats.

- *external* - this threat is one that involves factors outside of our control such as encountering a lion, being fired, being the victim of a rumor, or a relationship ending without our consent. The fear from this type of threat is that outside factors will cause something bad or unpleasant to happen.

- *internal* - this threat is one that involves physical sensations within our body such as rapid heartbeat, perspiration, shortness of breath, heart palpitations, muscle tension, etc.

- *phobias* - this threat usually involves a person, place or thing and even internal experiences not really harmful, but may be associated with the potential to harm. Some examples include heights, clowns, lizards, airplanes, dentists, elevators, driving, being in small, tight spaces, etc.

Read it again and give special attention to the 3 types of threats. We will pause here until tomorrow. Be sure to complete today's exercise and journal writing.

On Day 10, we will discover how the brain assesses potential threat or danger.

DAILY THOUGHT TRACKER

Identify and process automatic negative thoughts.

Day 9

OCCURRENCE

What happened?

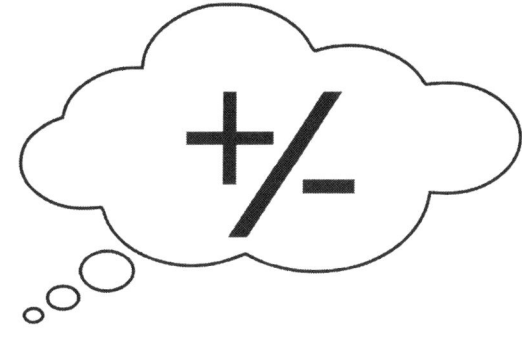

THOUGHTS

How did it make me feel?

EMOTIONS

What thoughts came up when the event was happening?

RESPONSE

What was my response to the situation?

SUPPORTIVE FACTORS

Why is my thought true?

NON-SUPPORTIVE FACTORS

Why might my thought not be true?

Understanding Anxiety and Its Impact

Instructions: Take a moment to reflect on what you read today and your thoughts today. Meditate on the scripture below and then journal or jot down notes you feel God is speaking to your heart.

Day 9 - Perceived Threat

"Therefore I tell you, do not be anxious about your life, what you will eat or what you will drink, nor about your body, what you will put on. Is not life more than food, and the body more than clothing?" Matt. 6:25

_____

_____

_____

_____

_____

_____

_____

_____

_____

_____

ASSESSMENT OF THREAT/DANGER - DAY 10

After fear kicks in, the mind begins to assess how "big" is this threat. In this step, the mind rations to determine how much danger you're in. Is the lizard big or small? Is the lizard coming in my direction? Is it going to jump on me?

Because the potential for danger is not immediate, your perception to the level or severity of the threat is often irrational and distorted. The mind works to determine when the actual danger (bad things) will happen - 1 minute, this afternoon, tomorrow, next week and so on. When you find yourself playing scenarios over and over again in your head with thoughts elevating your anxious state, this is called rumination. When rumination goes on and on and you are unable to turn it off, the ability to process rationally goes amiss.

Take a moment to think on a time when you found yourself ruminating about something that had you extremely anxious, but never happened or did not turn out like anything you had imagined? What did you realize from that experience? Reflect on it in your writing today.

Read it again and take mental notes. We will pause here until tomorrow. Be sure to complete today's exercise and journal writing.

On Day 11, we will learn about physiological and emotional responses to anxiety.

DAILY THOUGHT TRACKER

Identify and process automatic negative thoughts.

Day 10

OCCURRENCE

What happened?

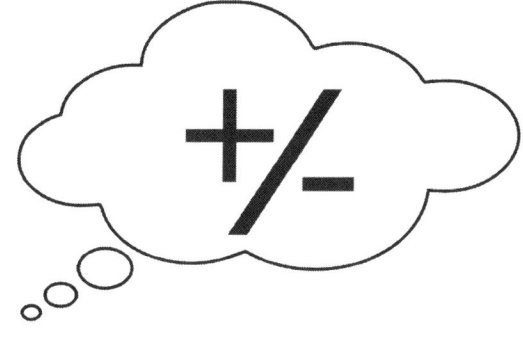

THOUGHTS

How did it make me feel?

EMOTIONS

What thoughts came up when the event was happening?

RESPONSE

What was my response to the situation?

SUPPORTIVE FACTORS

Why is my thought true?

NON-SUPPORTIVE FACTORS

Why might my thought not be true?

Understanding Anxiety and Its Impact

Instructions: Take a moment to reflect on what you read today and your thoughts today. Meditate on the scripture below and then journal or jot down notes you feel God is speaking to your heart.

Day 10 - Threat Assessment

"Cast your burden on the Lord, and he will sustain you; he will never permit the righteous to be moved." Psalm 55:22

_____

_____

_____

_____

_____

_____

_____

_____

_____

_____

PHYSIOLOGICAL AND EMOTIONAL RESPONSES - DAY 11

Fight or flight has been deemed the physiological response to threat (Cannon, 1915). We also have the *fawn or freeze* physiological responses (Walker, 2003). We have the parasympathetic nervous system and the sympathetic nervous system. The parasympathetic nervous system drives the *rest and digest* response and its primary purpose is to preserve energy for later use for bodily functioning such as digestion and urination (Tadi & Tindle, 2021). The sympathetic nervous system drives the *fight or flight* response in stressful or threatening situations. When the sympathetic nervous system activates, it sends a message to our pituitary glands to release a hormone known as ACTH and to the adrenal gland to release the neurotransmitter epinephrine (see illustration on page 48). When this happens, you may have:

- trembling

- elevated blood pressure

- shortness of breath

- rapid heartbeat

- heart palpitations

- perspiration

- rapid breathing

- constricted blood vessels

- tunnel vision or dilation of pupil

Again, these are all natural responses to when we perceive a threat or impending danger. They help us to survive and to determine whether our survival requires us to run away, defend ourselves, hold still/play dead or attempt to please.

It's important to note the brain and central nervous system work simultaneously. So as the body begins to react to a threat, parts of your brain are also at work in preparation of an emotional response. The two responses of the brain are either fear (it is happening now) or anxiety (it may happen in the future). God's purpose for creating instinctual fear was to provide us with an instantaneous response to increase survival. However, anxiety creates false alarms that trigger painful body sensations and arousals that causes us to run, avoid, or distract ourselves from what isn't dangerous. When we find ourselves riddled with anxiety, the enemy will often use it as a stronghold in our lives to prevent us from living an abundant, victorious life.

How has anxiety prevented you from living an abundant, victorious life? Reflect on it in your writings today.

We will pause here until tomorrow. Be sure to complete today's exercise and journal writing.

On Day 12, we will explore behavioral responses to anxiety.

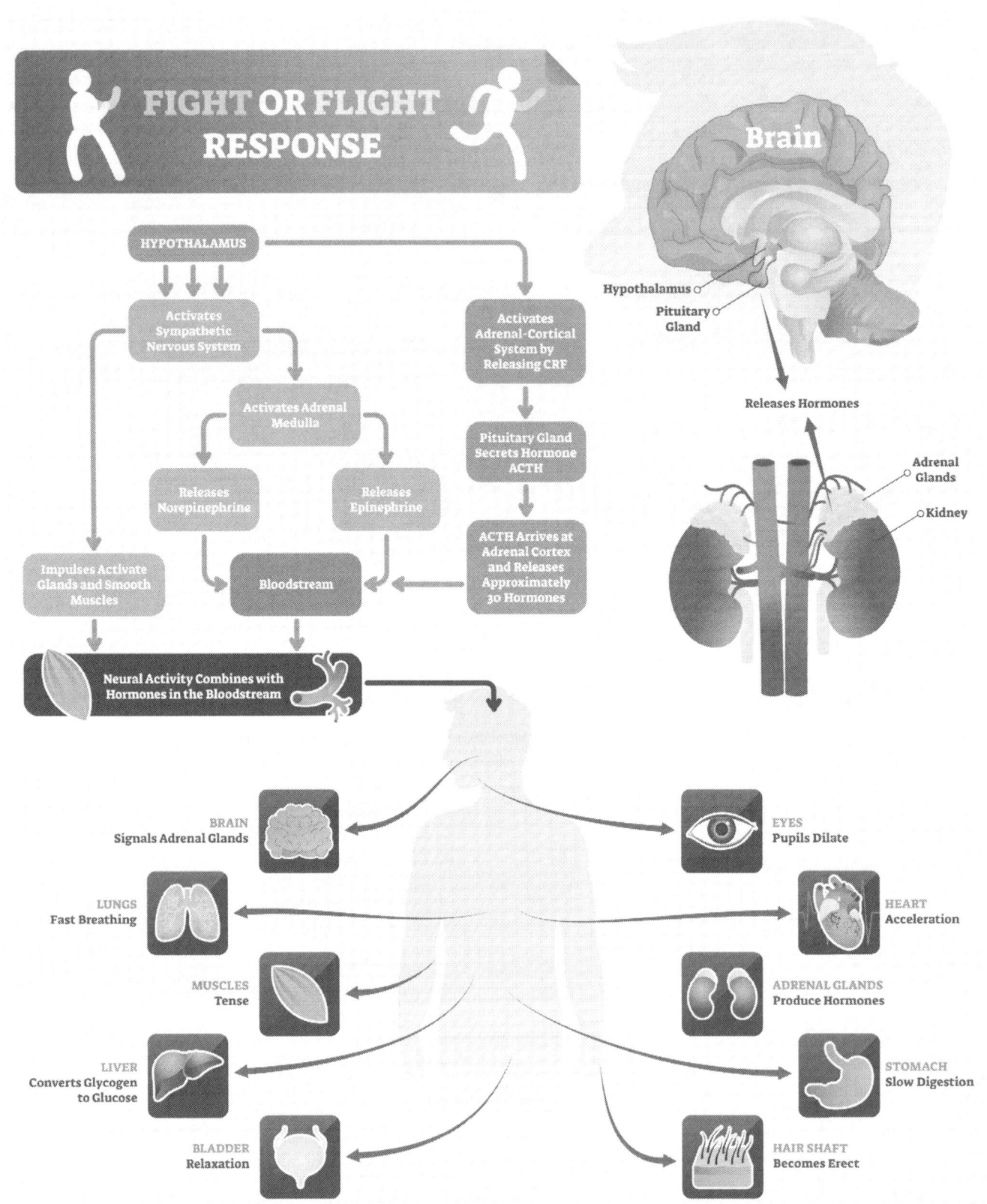

DAILY THOUGHT TRACKER

Identify and process automatic negative thoughts.

Day 11

OCCURRENCE

What happened?

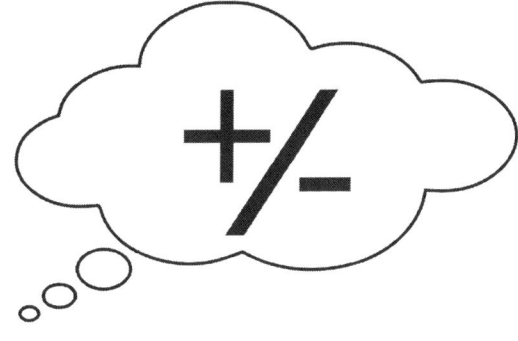

THOUGHTS

How did it make me feel?

EMOTIONS

What thoughts came up when the event was happening?

RESPONSE

What was my response to the situation?

SUPPORTIVE FACTORS

Why is my thought true?

NON-SUPPORTIVE FACTORS

Why might my thought not be true?

Understanding Anxiety and Its Impact

Instructions: Take a moment to reflect on what you read today and your thoughts today. Meditate on the scripture below and then journal or jot down notes you feel God is speaking to your heart.

Day 11 - Physical and Emotional Responses

"Peace I leave with you; my peace I give to you. Not as the world gives do I give to you. Let not your hearts be troubled, neither let them be afraid." John 14:27

_____

_____

_____

_____

_____

_____

_____

_____

_____

_____

_____

_____

_____

_____

_____

_____

_____

_____

_____

_____

_____

_____

BEHAVIORAL RESPONSES - DAY 12

Anger, fear and sadness are all emotions experienced as an attempt to protect us from what we view as threatening or harmful. They each require some type of response or call to action. For instance, anger arises when we feel we are being wronged, judged, and/or misunderstood. It drives how we respond to what we pose as a threat or an attack. Fear calls for us to quickly respond to prevent the threat or danger from happening. Sadness pushes us to sit with our own thoughts and process how a threat of loss or impending danger impacts us.

Examples of Behavioral Responses
Take a look at the list below to identify other behavioral responses linked to anxiety, but are often dismissed or overlooked.

- Restlessness
- Physical Tension
- Tremors
- Startle Reactions
- Rapid Speech
- Accident Proneness
- Interpersonal Withdrawal
- Inhibition
- Avoidance
- Flight
- Hyperventilation

Do you recognize any of these responses in yourself? Write about them today. We will pause here until tomorrow. Be sure to complete today's exercise and journal writing.

On Day 13, we will review an example of behavioral responses.

DAILY THOUGHT TRACKER

Identify and process automatic negative thoughts.

Day 12

OCCURRENCE

What happened?

THOUGHTS

How did it make me feel?

EMOTIONS

What thoughts came up when the event was happening?

RESPONSE

What was my response to the situation?

SUPPORTIVE FACTORS

Why is my thought true?

NON-SUPPORTIVE FACTORS

Why might my thought not be true?

Understanding Anxiety and Its Impact

Instructions: Take a moment to reflect on what you read today and your thoughts today. Meditate on the scripture below and then journal or jot down notes you feel God is speaking to your heart.

Day 12 - Behavioral Responses

"I can do all things through him who gives me strength." Phil. 4:13

_____

_____

_____

_____

_____

_____

_____

_____

_____

_____

BEHAVIORAL RESPONSES (EXAMPLE) - DAY 13

On Day 12 we learned what behavioral responses are and how they impact our daily functioning. Today, we are going to focus on understanding behavioral responses more clearly.

Let's take a look at an example.

Mike's Threat of Rejection (Example) - DAY 13

'As Mike is shopping, he sees two of his closest friends leaving a local coffee shop and heading across the street to the movie theater. Mike had spoken to both of them the previous day and neither mentioned they'd be spending time together. Mike began to feel a sunken feeling in the pit of his stomach and a feeling of terror gripped him (*perception of threat*). He began to think they were angry with him, didn't like him and did this to purposely hurt him (*assessment of threat*). Mike's heart began to race and he felt a rush of emotions of sadness, anger and fear (*physiological and emotional*). Mike's eyes began to fill with tears (*physiological and emotional*) as he thought over and over again what a terrible person he was and how did he ever think he would be good enough to be accepted by them (*assessment of threat*).

From childhood, Mike's parents often left him home alone and when they were home, they often sent him to his room or outside to play with friends. Mike felt alone and unwanted. Mike then tied these thoughts and feelings of loneliness and rejection to every relationship. Developing healthy and lasting relationships with friends was difficult for him.

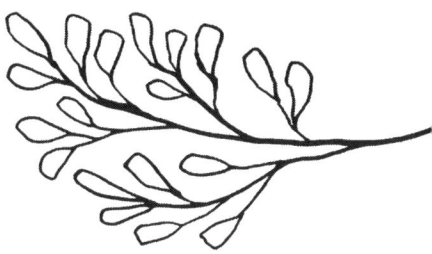

Anxiety consumed him because he struggled with self-love and receiving love from others. Mike never saw himself as a person others desired to be around, so he often found himself fawning (people-pleasing) to stay in relationship and to be accepted by others (*behavioral*). Mike began thinking of all the ways he could get his friends to involve him in every outing. He quickly realized this was out of his control and he began to feel alone again. Mike ruminated about his friends spending time together and speaking ill of him in his absence. As the ruminating continued, Mike became angrier, more anxious and decided he would not be speaking to either friend for awhile (*behavioral*). When his friends called later that evening and in the days that followed, Mike did not answer, but used avoidance as his coping mechanism to feel safe (*behavioral*).'

From this example, we see all four stages of anxiety at play. These four stages will continue to fuel anxiety if left unchecked. The next two chapters will focus on how you can begin to reclaim your life and no longer be bound to anxiety and its pain. You have the power to be free through God's Word and the tools you will learn about in Chapter 4.

> *We will conclude with a Check-In exercise on Day 14. Remember to complete all daily exercises and reflective journaling before moving on to Chapter 3.*

DAILY THOUGHT TRACKER

Identify and process automatic negative thoughts.

Day 13

OCCURRENCE
What happened?

THOUGHTS
How did it make me feel?

EMOTIONS
What thoughts came up when the event was happening?

RESPONSE
What was my response to the situation?

SUPPORTIVE FACTORS
Why is my thought true?

NON-SUPPORTIVE FACTORS
Why might my thought not be true?

Understanding Anxiety and Its Impact

Instructions: Take a moment to reflect on the example you read today and your thoughts today. Meditate on the scripture below and then journal or jot down notes you feel God is speaking to your heart.

Day 13 - Mike's Story

"Now may the Lord of peace himself give you peace at all times in every way. The Lord be with you all." II Thess. 3:16

_____

_____

_____

_____

_____

_____

_____

_____

_____

_____

ANXIETY AND ITS IMPACT RECAP - DAY 14

The purpose of this chapter is to shed light on anxiety and its internal and external impact. This chapter provided a description of how the brain and central nervous system work hand-in-hand and how anxiety triggers may send the central nervous system into fight or flight mode.

There are four key stages of anxiety we explored:

1. *Perception of threat/danger* - fear kicks in.

2. *Assessment of threat/danger* - you determine how serious the threat is and if you have the necessary resources to cope.

3. *Psychological and emotional responses* - you feel different physical sensations within the body to deal with the threat/danger and the feeling of fear, itself.

4. *Behavioral response* - You do something to deal with the threat such as facing it, avoiding it, or distracting yourself, etc.

These four stages will continue to fuel your anxiety if left unchecked.

Now, let's see what you've learned.

Check-in Time:
Understanding Anxiety Recap
Day 14

1. What are 3 things I learned in this chapter about anxiety that I did not know before related to fear vs anxiety, perceived threat and/or threat assessment and responses?

_____

_____

_____

2. What physiological and emotional responses have I identified about my response to anxiety?

_____

_____

_____

3. What behavioral responses do I recognize about myself when it comes to anxiety?

_____

_____

_____

DAILY THOUGHT TRACKER

Identify and process automatic negative thoughts.

Day 14

OCCURRENCE

What happened?

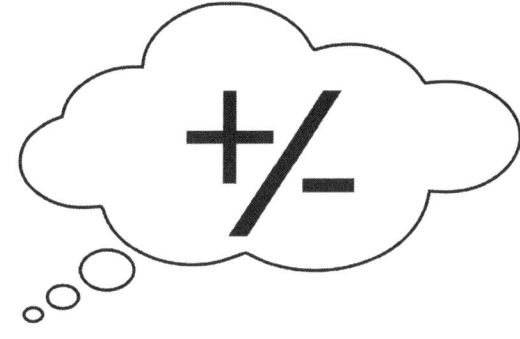

THOUGHTS

How did it make me feel?

EMOTIONS

What thoughts came up when the event was happening?

RESPONSE

What was my response to the situation?

SUPPORTIVE FACTORS

Why is my thought true?

NON-SUPPORTIVE FACTORS

Why might my thought not be true?

Understanding Anxiety and Its Impact

Instructions: Take a moment to reflect on the information and exercises and what you've learned overall in this chapter. Meditate on the scripture and confess aloud the affirmation below and listen as God speaks to your heart.

Day 14 - Reflective Journaling

"So we say with confidence, 'The Lord is my helper; I will not be afraid. What can mere mortals do to me?' " Heb. 13:6

"I have the power to overcome anxiety and I will not allow it to overcome me."

_____

_____

_____

_____

_____

_____

_____

WEEK 2 SCRIPTURE REFLECTIONS

Instructions: Continue meditating on these scriptures throughout your day and the weeks to come.

"For God gave us a spirit not of fear but of power and love and self-control." **II Tim. 1:7**

"Therefore I tell you, do not be anxious about your life, what you will eat or what you will drink, nor about your body, what you will put on. Is not life more than food, and the body more than clothing?"

Matt. 6:25

"Cast your burden on the Lord, and he will sustain you; he will never permit the righteous to be moved." **Psalm 55:22**

"Peace I leave with you; my peace I give to you. Not as the world gives do I give to you. Let not your hearts be troubled, neither let them be afraid." **John 14:27**

"I can do all this through him who gives me strength." **Phil. 4:13**

"Now may the Lord of peace himself give you peace at all times in every way. The Lord be with you all." **II Thess. 3:16**

"So we say with confidence, 'The Lord is my helper; I will not be afraid. What can mere mortals do to me?' " **Heb. 13:6**

CHAPTER

03

OVERCOMING ANXIETY AND STRESS WITH GOD'S WORD

Week 3: God's Word is the Final Authority

Overcoming Anxiety and Stress
Devotional

Stress usually occurs when we feel as though things are out of our control, there is change or a challenge arises. Much like fear, our bodies have been designed to naturally experience and react to stress by producing physical, emotional and mental responses. We know stressors will arise and that everything will not always be easy. However, we can look at challenges as reasons to gripe and complain or as opportunities to glorify God. That's totally up to us. I encourage you to choose the latter.

When we choose to let unexpected challenges, changes or circumstances serve as justification for complaining, we create an atmosphere for increased and ongoing anxiety. Life and death are by products to the words we speak. Learning dependence on God, accepting our limitations, and prayerfully considering decisions help us manage the stressors we encounter in every day life.

One major stressor that fuels anxiety is the inability to say no. God's Word instructs us to let our 'Yes' be 'Yes' and our 'No' be 'No' because anything else is from the evil one (Matt. 5:37).

What we say yes and no to should not be a matter of whim or peer pressure. We should prayerfully seek God's will in each day, and also in each season (we may need to change at times out of our comfortable routines). God has given us spiritual gifts to serve others, but we cannot be all or do all.

So how do we combat stress to overcome anxiety? By learning what it truly means to rest. Rest is something many people choose only when their health forces them. Jesus sought times of solitude and what we would call "time to recharge" (See Mark 6:30-32, Luke 5:16, Luke 6:12-13). The need for rest routines can be a daily, weekly, and seasonal reminder that we all must rely on God's strength by casting our cares (stressors) upon Him (I Peter 5:7).

Managing stress means we will be free to say yes to the things we need to and say no to the things we need to, in order to walk with God in this season. Managing stress means evaluating priorities, letting God prune away things that are holding us back from using our time and resources wisely, and being intentional with everything He has given us. He will be glorified by the balanced life we lead as we surrender to His will and His leading through Holy Spirit and His Word.

Prayer

Father,

Thank you for the reassurance that I can lean on you for strength at any time. I am grateful to know I do not have to face anxiety and stress alone. I realize I have been trying to handle my stressors in my own strength and not seeking you for guidance, comfort and rest. Today, I choose to give you my cares. I know you are well able to take care of them and me. Father, today, I rest in You. In Jesus' name, Amen.

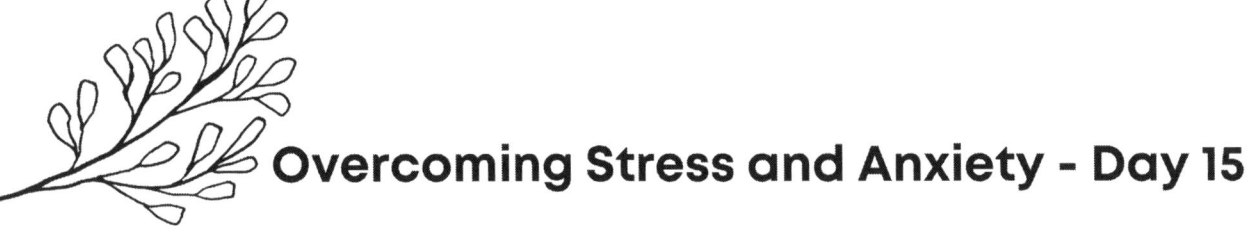

Overcoming Stress and Anxiety - Day 15

Instructions: Take a moment to answer the questions below to identify how stress influences anxiety.

1. What stress triggers have I identified that cause me to become anxious (i.e. loud noises, unexpected emails, over committing, etc).

_____

_____

_____

2. What signs and symptoms am I aware of that let me know I am stressed (physically, mentally and emotionally)?

_____

_____

_____

3. How do I usually respond to stress causing me to be anxious?

_____

_____

_____

Overcoming Anxiety and Stress

Instructions: Take a moment to reflect on the devotion you read today and your stressors today. Meditate on the scripture below and then journal or jot down notes you feel God is speaking to your heart.

Day 15 - Devotional Journaling

"Come to me, all who labor and are heavy laden, and I will give you rest. Take my yoke upon you, and learn from me, for I am gentle and lowly in heart, and you will find rest for your souls. For my yoke is easy, and my burden is light." Matt. 11:28-30

_____

_____

_____

_____

_____

_____

_____

_____

_____

Am I Stressed?
Stress Assessment Questionnaire
Day 16

Answer these questions below to see how you have been doing with responding to stressors. (This assessment is not meant to replace a clinical assessment).

Answer All Of The Following Questions: Yes or No

1. Do you tend to keep everything inside?
2. Do you frequently neglect exercise?
3. Do you have few supportive relationships?
4. Do you often get too little rest?
5. Do you frequently find yourself spending a lot of time complaining about the past?
6. Do you often ignore stress symptoms?
7. Do you frequently put things off until later?
8. Do you frequently complain that you are disorganized?
9. Do you often find yourself racing through the day?
10. Do you frequently try to do everything yourself?
11. Do you blow up easily and often?
12. Do you frequently seek unrealistic goals?
13. Do you frequently fail to see the humor in situations others find funny?
14. Do you frequently and easily get irritated?
15. Do you frequently seem to make a "big deal" of everything?

(continue to next page)

16. Do you often feel unable to cope with all you have to do?

17. Do you frequently think there is only one right way to do something?

18. Do you frequently get angry when you are kept waiting?

19. Do you frequently neglect your diet?

20. Do you often fail to build relaxation into every day?

Yes Answer = 1 Point

Understand Your Score

Scores of 1-6 = I'm Good

Scores of 7-12 = I'm Doing Okay

Scores of 13-17 = Things Are Challenging

Scores of 18+ = I'm Stressed Out and Need Change

*Total Score:*_____

Overcoming Anxiety and Stress

Instructions: Take a moment to reflect on your assessment scores and any stressors today. Meditate on the scripture below and then journal or jot down notes you feel God is speaking to your heart.

Day 16 - Stress Assessment

"When the righteous cry for help, the LORD hears and delivers them out of all their troubles." Psalm 34:17

_____

_____

_____

_____

_____

_____

_____

_____

_____

_____

"CLOUDY" THOUGHTS

Day 17

As you think about some of your stressors, consider the thoughts that accompany them. Then, in the clouds, write words to describe your stressful thoughts and feelings that cause anxiety.

Overcoming Anxiety and Stress

Instructions: Take a moment to reflect on the exercise today and any stressors today. Meditate on the scripture below and then journal or jot down notes you feel God is speaking to your heart.

Day 17 - Cloudy Thoughts

"Say to those who have an anxious heart, 'Be strong; fear not! Behold, your God will come with vengeance, with the recompense of God. He will come and save you.' " Isaiah 35:4

_____

_____

_____

_____

_____

_____

_____

_____

_____

THOUGHT AWARENESS
Day 18

Observe your mind and body as you think about a stressful situation. Do not suppress any thoughts. Let them run their course while you watch them, and write them down as they come.

The next step is to rationally challenge your negative thoughts. Check to see whether every thought you wrote down is reasonable.

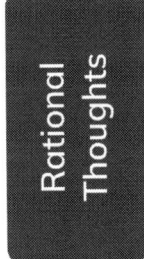

Use rational, positive thoughts and affirmations to counter negative thinking. See if there are any opportunities that are offered by it.

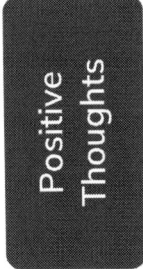

Overcoming Anxiety and Stress

Instructions: Take a moment to reflect on the exercise today and any triggers today. Meditate on the scripture below and then journal or jot down notes you feel God is speaking to your heart.

Day 18 - Thought Awareness

"And I am convinced that nothing can ever separate us from God's love. Neither death nor life, neither angels nor demons, neither our fears for today nor our worries about tomorrow—not even the powers of hell can separate us from God's love."
Romans 8:38-39

_____

_____

_____

_____

_____

_____

_____

_____

_____

Understanding
YOUR TRIGGERS
Day 19

Try to fill in what you recognize as triggers. Triggers are anything such as an event, experience or memory that causes an intense emotional reaction. You may begin to understand how stress influences anxiety better. Particularly what triggers may exist and how stress and anxiety follow.

Trigger(s)

Feelings

Thoughts

Physical Symptoms

Behaviors

Overcoming Anxiety and Stress

Instructions: Take a moment to reflect on the exercise today and any stressors today. Meditate on the scripture below and then journal or jot down notes you feel God is speaking to your heart.

Day 19 - Understanding Triggers

"For I know the plans I have for you,' declares the Lord, plans to prosper you and not to harm you, plans to give you hope and a future." Jer. 29:11

_____

_____

_____

_____

_____

_____

_____

_____

_____

_____

_____

_____

_____

_____

_____

_____

_____

_____

_____

_____

_____

_____

_____

_____

_____

ANXIETY & STRESS BODY SCAN
Day 20

Close your eyes. Take a deep breath in through your nose and out through your mouth. Envision a ball of light, starting with the top of your head, then notice how your body feels. Slowly move down your body with the ball of light, noticing how each body part feels, down to your toes. Make a note of any areas of discomfort on the body below. Draw a face on the person to represent how you are currently feeling. You may repeat this exercise daily.

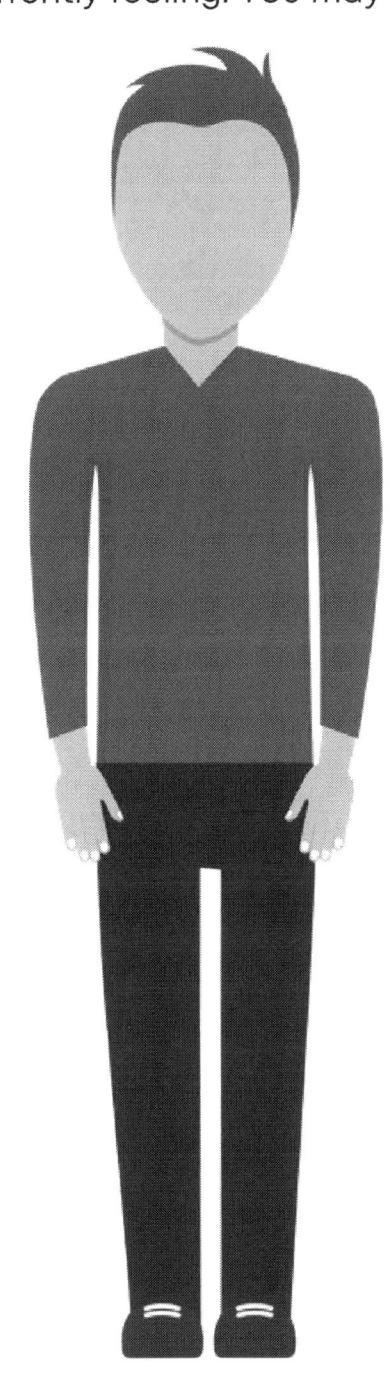

Overcoming Anxiety and Stress

Instructions: Take a moment to reflect on today's exercise and any stressors today. Meditate on the scripture below and then journal or jot down notes you feel God is speaking to your heart.

Day 20 -Body Scan

"So do not fear, for I am with you; do not be dismayed, for I am your God. I will strengthen you and help you; I will uphold you with my righteous right hand." Isaiah 41:10

_____

_____

_____

_____

_____

_____

_____

_____

_____

THOUGHT RESTRUCTURING

Day 21

Changing Your Thinking To Reduce Your Stress

Thought restructuring helps you understand what is behind negative emotions and moods. These negative influencers are known as *triggers*. When stress is triggered, anxiety usually follows.

Step 1: Identify the Event

Describe the situation that triggered your negative mood.

Step 2: Analyze How You Felt

Describe how you felt in the situation, and how you're feeling now.

Step 3: Identify Automatic Thoughts

Make a list of your automatic thoughts in response to the situation.

Step 4: Find Objective Evidence

Write down any evidence you can find that supports the automatic thoughts and any evidence that contradicts the thought.

Step 5: Monitor Your Present Feelings

Take a moment to assess your state of mind. Do you feel better about the event? Is there any action you need to take? Write down your present feelings, along with any further steps that you need to take.

Overcoming Anxiety and Stress

Instructions: Take a moment to reflect on the devotion, exercises and what you've learned overall in this chapter. Meditate on the scripture and confess aloud the affirmation below and listen as God speaks to your heart.

Day 21 - Reflective Journaling

"Have I not commanded you? Be strong and courageous. Do not be afraid; do not be discouraged, for the LORD your God will be with you wherever you go." Josh. 1:9

"I am purposing to live a life of peace by managing my stress and resting in God's Word."

_____

_____

_____

_____

_____

_____

_____

WEEK 3 SCRIPTURE REFLECTIONS

Instructions: Continue meditating on these scriptures throughout your day and in the weeks to come.

"Come to me, all who labor and are heavy laden, and I will give you rest. Take my yoke upon you, and learn from me, for I am gentle and lowly in heart, and you will find rest for your souls. For my yoke is easy, and my burden is light." **Matt. 11:28-30**

"When the righteous cry for help, the LORD hears and delivers them out of all their troubles." **Psalm 34:17**

"Say to those who have an anxious heart, 'Be strong; fear not! Behold, your God will come with vengeance, with the recompense of God. He will come and save you.' " **Isaiah 35:4**

"And I am convinced that nothing can ever separate us from God's love. Neither death nor life, neither angels nor demons, neither our fears for today nor our worries about tomorrow—not even the powers of hell can separate us from God's love." **Romans 8:38-39**

" 'For I know the plans I have for you,' declares the Lord, 'plans to prosper you and not to harm you, plans to give you hope and a future.' " **Jer. 29:11**

"So do not fear, for I am with you; do not be dismayed, for I am your God. I will strengthen you and help you; I will uphold you with my righteous right hand." **Isaiah 41:10**

"Have I not commanded you? Be strong and courageous. Do not be afraid; do not be discouraged, for the LORD your God will be with you wherever you go." **Josh. 1:9**

C H A P T E R

04

GOD'S WORD AND OTHER RESOURCES

Week 4: God's Word is the Final Authority

God's Word is the Final Authority
Devotional

Anxiety and stress are opposers to our faith as Christians. As life happens and unexpected challenges arise, we will always be faced with the war within our minds to either worry or remain steadfast in faith. In James 1:3 we are reminded that when our faith is tested, our endurance (patience) has the opportunity to grow.

But how can I grow in patience if anxiety and stress haunt me? How can I see my faith being tested as something positive when it (the test) makes me feel as though I am falling apart inside? James assures us that learning to grow in patience and learning to see a test of our faith as a positive is an ongoing process when he says in James 1:4 (Amp.) - "And let endurance have its perfect result and do a thorough work, so that you may be perfect and completely developed [in your faith], lacking in nothing."

It is important we give ourselves grace as we begin our journey of overcoming anxiety and learning how to manage stress effectively. Remember Psalm 94:19 (NIV), "When anxiety was great within me, your consolation brought me joy." Consolation here refers to God's comfort, love, reassurance, help and His soothing touch. We are able to experience God's consolation through His Word and through Holy Spirit.

Creating an intentional practice of not only reading, but studying, meditating, hearing and confessing God's Word daily will begin to build endurance within us and help to restructure our thought processes. Developing a daily prayer life where you declare God's Word and practice gratitude builds faith and confidence in who you are as a believer, who God is as your Father, and what His Word promises. Prov. 12:25 reads, "Anxiety weighs down the heart, but a kind word cheers it up." As you begin to declare God's Word, anticipate Holy Spirit ministering to your heart and lifting your spirits.

No matter what we face, as believers, we must rest in this truth - God's Word is the **FINAL** authority in our lives! This means that despite our challenges and our anxieties, we trust (hold fast to with confidence) what God's Word has declared because we believe it will manifest in our lives. What God's Word says about us, our circumstances and our future is what we should put our energy, focus, and hope in. After all, His track record is our undeniable evidence that His Word works.

Prayer

Father,

I am grateful to know that despite my struggles with anxiety and stress Your consolation is always available to minister to my heart and soul. I realize life will continue to happen and I am thankful that I take hope in Your Word being the final authority in my life. I trust that You have already mapped out the days of my life and they are filled with hope and lasting joy. I choose to rest in this truth. In Jesus' name, Amen.

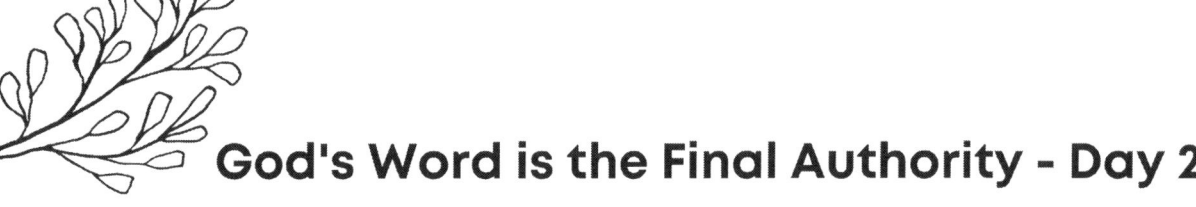

God's Word is the Final Authority - Day 22

Instructions: Take a moment to answer the questions below to identify how you can take steps to overcome anxiety and stress.

1. How has anxiety and stress impacted my ability to trust God and His Word?

_____

_____

_____

2. What 3 things did I take from the devotion that I can begin applying right now?

_____

_____

_____

3. How may I allow God's Word to be the final authority in my life when it comes to anxiety?

_____

_____

_____

God's Word is the Final Authority

Instructions: Take a moment to reflect on the devotion and the exercise that followed. Meditate on the scripture below and then journal or jot down notes you feel God is speaking to your heart.

Day 22 - Devotional Journaling

"Trust in the LORD with all your heart and lean not on your own understanding; in all your ways submit to him, and he will make your paths straight." Prov. 3:5-6

_____

_____

_____

_____

_____

_____

_____

_____

_____

_____

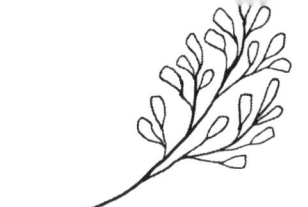

How to Overcome Anxiety
Day 23

Throughout this workbook we have learned how anxiety challenges our faith, a deeper understanding of anxiety and our responses, and that no matter what - God's Word is our FINAL authority.

Now, how do we tie this all together and overcome anxiety? The answer is two-fold. You can:

- Keep avoiding what you fear or
- Stop avoiding what you fear.

We know it isn't that simple, but the longer you avoid, the more entrapped by fear and anxiety your life becomes. Also, solutions such as medication management alone and relying on others solely for support aren't always permanent solutions. We have to discredit the belief that the thing(s) we fear will cause harm to us. The way we do this is through exposure - facing or doing the very thing we fear.

There are two types of exposures I'll introduce to you here. One is contact exposure - being present with or near the very thing you believe will harm you; and imagery exposure - visiting a memory of the very thing you experienced before that caused you anxiety or you imagining the very thing you fear in the future causing you anxiety now. Exposure sometimes requires the support of a trained mental health professional.

Severe, debilitating anxiety may also require the support of a trained mental health professional to determine whether biological, neurological and/or genetic factors are the source.

Beyond exposure is the need for routine self-care - intentionally engaging in practices that promote mental, emotional and physical health.

Check out the self-care exercise on the next page.

Self-care Checklist
FOR ANXIETY *Day 23*

Instructions: Below is an example of how to complete the self-care checklist. On the following page is a blank one for you to complete.

wake up
early

pray

eat healthy

love

laugh

stretch &
exercise

Self-care Checklist
FOR ANXIETY
Day 23

Instructions: Fill in each circle with an action you will take each day to reduce anxiety and improve overall functioning.

God's Word is the Final Authority

Instructions: Take a moment to reflect on today's exercise and any anxiety that you experienced today. Meditate on the scripture below and then journal or jot down notes you feel God is speaking to your heart.

Day 23 - Self-Care Reflection

"But blessed is the one who trusts in the LORD, whose confidence is in him. They will be like a tree planted by the water that sends out its roots by the stream. It does not fear when heat comes; its leaves are always green. It has no worries in a year of drought and never fails to bear fruit."
Jer. 17:7-8

_____

_____

_____

_____

_____

_____

_____

GOALS

Day 24

FOR EACH OF THE CATEGORIES BELOW, WRITE DOWN WHAT YOU ARE DOING WELL AND WHERE YOU NEED IMPROVEMENT. TAKE THE TIME TO REFLECT ON THESE, AND WRITE A GOAL FOR EACH CATEGORY TO REDUCE ANXIETY.

CATEGORY	DOING WELL	NEEDS IMPROVEMENT	GOALS
FAMILY			
FRIENDS			
WORK/ SCHOOL			
BODY			
MENTAL HEALTH			
FAITH			

God's Word is the Final Authority

Instructions: Take a moment to reflect on today's exercise and any stressors today. Meditate on the scripture below and then journal or jot down notes you feel God is speaking to your heart.

Day 24 - Well Goals

"When I am afraid, I put my trust in you." Psalm 56:3

_____

_____

_____

_____

_____

_____

_____

_____

_____

_____

_____

GRATITUDE
Day 25

Instructions: Take a moment to make a list of all you are grateful for.

TODAY I'M GRATEFUL FOR...

_____

_____

_____

_____

_____

_____

_____

_____

_____

_____

_____

_____

_____

_____

_____

God's Word is the Final Authority

Instructions: Take a moment to reflect on today's gratitude exercise and anything that happened to challenge your thankfulness today. Meditate on the scripture below and then journal or jot down notes you feel God is speaking to your heart.

Day 25 - Gratitude

"Let the peace of Christ rule in your hearts, since as members of one body you were called to peace. And be thankful." Col. 3:15

_____

_____

_____

_____

_____

_____

_____

_____

_____

TASK DUMPING
LET'S DO IT.
Day 26

Task dumping (brain dumping) allows you to get all of your tasks out of your head and onto paper without having to think in detail. It is a way to allow the brain to be free of stressful thinking.

Rate what level of priority each task holds:

H stands for High priority
M stands for Medium priority
L stands for Low priority

Here's one example:

TASKS	PRIORITY			COMPLETED
Respond to urgent emails.	(✓)	(M)	(L)	( )
Go to the gym.	(H)	(✓)	(L)	( )
Call a friend back to chat	(H)	(M)	(✓)	( )

TASK DUMPING
Day 26

TASKS	PRIORITY			COMPLETED
_____	(H)	(M)	(L)	◯
_____	(H)	(M)	(L)	◯
_____	(H)	(M)	(L)	◯
_____	(H)	(M)	(L)	◯
_____	(H)	(M)	(L)	◯
_____	(H)	(M)	(L)	◯
_____	(H)	(M)	(L)	◯
_____	(H)	(M)	(L)	◯
_____	(H)	(M)	(L)	◯
_____	(H)	(M)	(L)	◯
_____	(H)	(M)	(L)	◯
_____	(H)	(M)	(L)	◯
_____	(H)	(M)	(L)	◯
_____	(H)	(M)	(L)	◯

God's Word is the Final Authority

Instructions: Take a moment to reflect on today's exercise and how it was helpful. Meditate on the scripture below and then journal or jot down notes you feel God is speaking to your heart.

Day 26 - Task Dumping

"I sought the LORD, and he answered me; he delivered me from all my fears." Psalm 34:4

_____

_____

_____

_____

_____

_____

_____

_____

_____

_____

2 Mindfulness Techniques to Help With Anxiety

Day 27

Mindfulness Through Prayer

There are three layers to developing mindful prayer. The first is simply a mindful acknowledgement throughout each day that God is with us. Because God is fully present in every moment, simple awareness of our experience creates opportunities for unending prayers. The next layer is formal meditation. The silence and open stance of mindfulness meditation creates a deeper awareness of God, softening our resistance to His voice. The third layer is even deeper. This layer includes an intentional awareness of God's presence with us. Sit quietly and meditate on knowing God is present with you and in you for 5-10 mins.

Mindfulness Through Breathwork (4-7-8 Breathing)

1. Sit upright in a chair or cross-legged (see illustration) on a floor.
2. Empty your lungs of air.
3. Breathe in through your nose for 4 seconds, hold your breath for 7 seconds, exhale out of your mouth for 8 seconds.
4. Repeat at least 4 times.

www.chanellfinley.com

God's Word is the Final Authority

Instructions: Take a moment to reflect on today's exercises and process whether you believe mindfulness is helpful. Meditate on the scripture below and then journal or jot down notes you feel God is speaking to your heart.

Day 27 - Prayer and Breath Mindfulness

"Finally, Be strong in the Lord and in the strength of His might. Put on the whole armor of God, that you may be able to stand against the wiles of the devil." Eph. 6:10-11

_____

_____

_____

_____

_____

_____

_____

_____

_____

Check Your
THINKING
Day 28

REVIEW THE LIFE AREAS LISTED BELOW AND RATE YOURSELF BETWEEN 1-10
WITH HOW SELF-AWARE AND CONFIDENT YOU ARE IN EACH CATEGORY.

CONFIDENT IN YOURSELF

1   2   3   4   5   6   7   8   9   10

VERY LITTLE   VERY MUCH

ABLE TO BE POSITIVE

1   2   3   4   5   6   7   8   9   10

VERY LITTLE   VERY MUCH

ADAPTABLE ATTITUDE

1   2   3   4   5   6   7   8   9   10

VERY LITTLE   VERY MUCH

SOUND DECISION-MAKING

1   2   3   4   5   6   7   8   9   10

VERY LITTLE   VERY MUCH

CAPABLE OF STAYING ON TASK WITH GOALS

1   2   3   4   5   6   7   8   9   10

VERY LITTLE   VERY MUCH

www.chanellfinley.com

God's Word is the Final Authority

Instructions: Take a moment to reflect on today's exercise and your thinking. Meditate on the scripture below and then journal or jot down notes you feel God is speaking to your heart.

Day 28 - Thinking Check

"Examine me, God! Look at my heart! Put me to the test! Know my anxious thoughts!" Psalm 139:23 CEB

_____

_____

_____

_____

_____

_____

_____

_____

_____

_____

ANXIETY & STRESS
CHECKLIST Day 29

AS YOU READ EACH QUESTION, SIMPLY CHECK "YES" IF YOU AGREE OR "NO" IF YOU DISAGREE WITH THE STATEMENT. RESPOND BASED ON WHAT HAS OCCURRED OVER THE LAST MONTH.

		YES	NO
01	IN THE LAST MONTH I HAVE BEEN MORE ANXIOUS THAN USUAL.	☐	☐
02	MY STRESSORS HAVE REMAINED THE SAME.	☐	☐
03	MY THOUGHTS REMAIN MORE NEGATIVE THAN POSITIVE.	☐	☐
04	WHEN I BECOME ANXIOUS I USUALLY ISOLATE, STRESS EAT AND/OR BECOME EASILY IRRITABLE.	☐	☐
05	WHEN I AM STRESSED, I AM UNABLE TO SLEEP OR REST.	☐	☐
06	I USUALLY FIND A NEGATIVE MEANS TO COPE WHEN ANXIOUS OR STRESSED.	☐	☐
07	I AM HOPEFUL I CAN MANAGE AND OVERCOME ANXIETY.	☐	☐
08	I TRY TO CONSISTENTLY USE POSITIVE COPING SKILLS TO REDUCE ANXIETY AND STRESS.	☐	☐

God's Word is the Final Authority

Instructions: Take a moment to reflect on the checklist and what you learned today. Jot down what stood out to you and what spoke to your heart.

Day 29 - Anxiety & Stress Checklist

"But those who hope in the Lord will renew their strength; they will fly up on wings like eagles; they will run and not be tired; they will walk and not be weary." Isaiah 40:31

_____

_____

_____

_____

_____

_____

_____

_____

_____

Anxiety
COPING LIST
Day 30

FILL IN THE CHECKLIST SPACES BELOW WITH SELF-CARE ACTIVITIES THAT YOU
CAN DO IN THE MORNING AND AT EVENING TO COMBAT ANXIETY.

MORNING SELF-CARE

- ○ _____
- ○ _____
- ○ _____
- ○ _____
- ○ _____
- ○ _____
- ○ _____
- ○ _____

EVENING SELF-CARE

- ○ _____
- ○ _____
- ○ _____
- ○ _____
- ○ _____
- ○ _____
- ○ _____
- ○ _____

God's Word is the Final Authority

Instructions: Take a moment to reflect on the coping list and what you learned today. Jot down what stood out to you and what spoke to your heart.

Day 30 - Coping with Anxiety

"Turn from evil and do good; seek peace and pursue it. The eyes of the Lord are on the righteous, and his ears are attentive to their cry." Psalm 34:14-15

_____

_____

_____

_____

_____

_____

_____

_____

_____

IMPORTANT? Day 31

RANK THE TOP 10 MOST IMPORTANT THINGS IN YOUR LIFE AND ESTIMATE HOW MUCH TIME YOU SPEND ON THEM WEEKLY. DOING WHAT MATTERS MOST HELPS TO REDUCE ANXIETY.

IMPORTANT THINGS IN YOUR LIFE

01 _____

02 _____

03 _____

04 _____

05 _____

06 _____

07 _____

08 _____

09 _____

10 _____

WRITE YOUR REFLECTIVE NOTES IN THE *REFLECTIVE JOURNALING* SECTION.

GRATITUDE
Day 31

/ /

TAKEAWAYS FOR THE MONTH

1 _____

2 _____

3 _____

SHARE WHAT YOU HAVE LEARNED NEW

_____

_____

_____

SHARE SOME OF THE DIFFICULTIES YOU ENCOUNTERED

_____

_____

_____

SHARE WHAT YOU'VE DONE FOR YOURSELF THIS MONTH

_____

_____

_____

HAS PRACTICING DAILY GRATITUDE HELPED WITH ANXIETY THIS MONTH?

| YES | MAYBE | NO |

*Master copy located in Additional Resources for ongoing monthly reviews

God's Word is the Final Authority

Instructions: Take a moment to reflect on the information and exercises and what you've learned from this entire workbook. Reflect on the scripture and confess aloud the affirmation below and listen as God speaks to your heart.

Day 31 - Reflective Journaling

"You will keep in perfect and constant peace the one whose mind is steadfast [that is, committed and focused on You—in both inclination and character], Because he trusts and takes refuge in You [with hope and confident expectation]." Isaiah 26:3 AMP

"I am fully equipped to overcome anxiety with God's Word and the resources I now have."

_____

_____

_____

_____

_____

_____

_____

WEEK 4 SCRIPTURE REFLECTIONS

Instructions: Continue meditating on these scriptures throughout your day and the weeks to come.

"Trust in the LORD with all your heart and lean not on your own understanding; in all your ways submit to him, and he will make your paths straight." **Prov. 3:5-6**

"But blessed is the one who trusts in the LORD, whose confidence is in him. They will be like a tree planted by the water that sends out its roots by the stream. It does not fear when heat comes; its leaves are always green. It has no worries in a year of drought and never fails to bear fruit." **Jer. 17:7-8**

"When I am afraid, I put my trust in you." **Psalm 56:3**

"Let the peace of Christ rule in your hearts, since as members of one body you were called to peace. And be thankful." **Col. 3:15**

"I sought the LORD, and he answered me; he delivered me from all my fears." **Psalm 34:4**

"Finally, Be strong in the Lord and in the strength of His might. Put on the whole armor of God, that you may be able to stand against the wiles of the devil." **Eph. 6:10-11**

"Examine me, God! Look at my heart! Put me to the test! Know my anxious thoughts!" **Psalm 139:23 CEB**

"But those who hope in the Lord will renew their strength; they will fly up on wings like eagles; they will run and not be tired; they will walk and not be weary." **Isaiah 40:31**

"Turn from evil and do good; seek peace and pursue it. The eyes of the Lord are on the righteous, and his ears are attentive to their cry." **Psalm 34:14-15**

"You will keep in perfect and constant peace the one whose mind is steadfast [that is, committed and focused on You—in both inclination and character], Because he trusts and takes refuge in You [with hope and confident expectation]." **Isaiah 26:3 AMP**

ANXIETY POST ASSESSMENT SCREENER

The post assessment below is the same as the preassessment screener. Retake the screener below and compare your score to your prescreener score at the beginning of this workbook. Note whether your score has decreased or increased. Then continue utilizing the techniques learned in this workbook to continue combatting anxiety and stress.

Anxiety Screen Questionnaire

GAD-7				
Over the last 2 weeks, how often have you been bothered by the following problems? *(Use "√" to indicate your answer)*	Not at all	Several days	More than half the days	Nearly every day
1. Feeling nervous, anxious or on edge	0	1	2	3
2. Not being able to stop or control worrying	0	1	2	3
3. Worrying too much about different things	0	1	2	3
4. Trouble relaxing	0	1	2	3
5. Being so restless that it is hard to sit still	0	1	2	3
6. Becoming easily annoyed or irritable	0	1	2	3
7. Feeling afraid as if something awful might happen	0	1	2	3

Scoring:

☐ 5 – 9 Mild anxiety

☐ 10 – 14 Moderate anxiety

☐ 15 – 21 Severe anxiety

Total Score T_____ = _____ + _____ + _____

You Did It!

This concludes our 31-day devotional workbook. I hope you have gained a greater understanding of what God's Word says about you, about anxiety and how you can overcome. Also, I hope you've acquired important knowledge on anxiety and its impact in your life. Please continue to use the techniques learned within this workbook and to reuse all of the activities and exercises as you deem necessary.

Also, remember this workbook is no way intended to take the place of therapy, mental health treatment, medication management or seeking needed help from a trained professional. Rather, it is an additional resource to aid in healing and growth.

If you find that after implementing the tools and resources made available here, you still are not able to overcome anxiety, please consider seeking professional help from a licensed mental health professional.

For continued practice and implementation of what has been covered in this workbook, I have created the *12-Day Anxiety Breakers Challenge*. Each day of the challenge you are prompted to do a different task to manage anxiety and stress. It follows this page.

My continued prayer for you is that you grow in the knowledge of who you are in Christ, your authority and power given by Him and the predestined victory you have because of Him.

In Faith & Wellness,

12 Days of
Anxiety Breakers Challenge

1 Pray with Gratitude

2 Focus on Your Breath Throughout The Day

3 Give Praise to God for His Goodness

4 Say 3 Positive Things About Yourself

5 Give Thanks For People You Love

6 List Awesome Things That Happened Today

7 Visualize A Place of Peace for 2 Mins

8 Take A Few Breaths Outside

9 Recite 3 Scriptures On Who God Says You Are

10 List 10 Things You Are Grateful For

11 Say 3 Positive Affirmations About Your Day

12 Allow Yourself 3 Mins to Sit with Anxious Thoughts

CERTIFICATE

OF ACHIEVEMENT

Anxiety Breaker

PROUDLY PRESENTED TO

A Man of Faith

because of his self-determination to do the work to overcome anxiety and stress. You are deserving of a life filled with joy, peace and God's goodness. May this certificate be an ongoing reminder.

Chanell Finley, M.Ed. LPC-S

**EMOTIONAL WELLNESS
MENTOR**

P O S T
E X E R C I S E S

EXTRAS

ADDITIONAL RESOURCES

God's Word is the Final Authority

_____

Affirmations

I am learning how to express myself and speak my wants, needs and desires.

I am shifting my energy from fear to love because perfect love casts out fear.

I am in control of my emotions and no longer allow my emotions to control me.

I am taking life one day at a time and not allowing anxiety to steal my joy.

I am maturing emotionally and I am making healthier decisions that make my life easier.

I am no longer bound or stuck by old patterns of behavior because Christ set me free.

I am creating a place within and outwardly that exudes peace, strength and hope.

I am powerful and have all authority over the worries I face each day.

I am focusing on right now and leaning into peace, excitement and rest.

I am intentional because God is bringing to pass my heart's desires.

I am prioritizing my relationship with God, with self and with others to continue in peace and hope.

MY CHECKLIST TO REDUCE ANXIETY

- ✓ Pray Throughout My Day

- ✓ 5 Minute Deep Breathing

- ✓ Exercise

- ✓ Take a 30 Minute Walk/Jog

TRIANGULAR BREATHING
ANXIETY BREAK

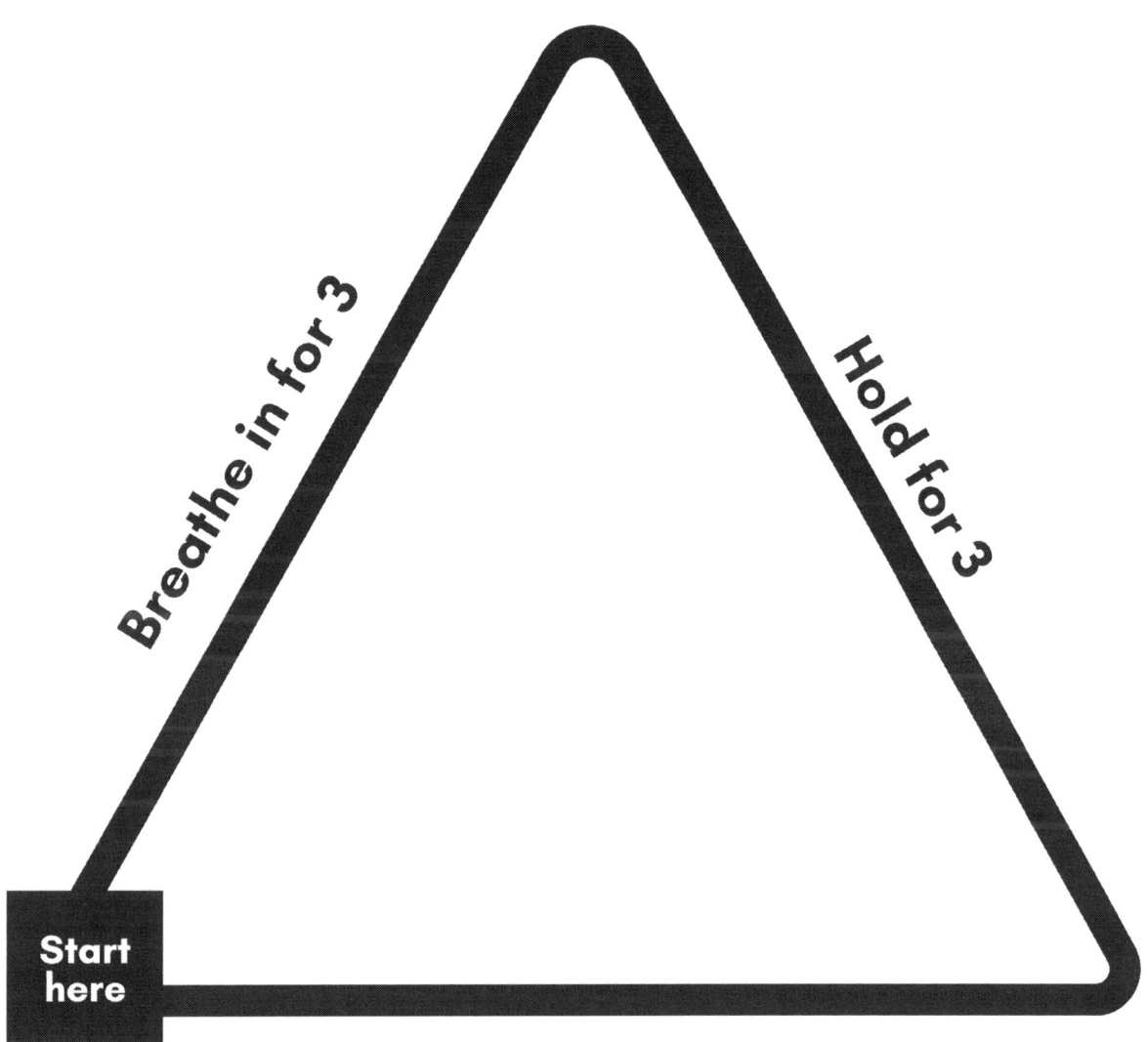

Starting at the left bottom of the triangle.Trace your finger up the side while you take a deep breath in. Hold your breath for three seconds as you slide down the other side. Breathe out along the bottom of the triangle. Repeat it until you are calm.

ASSESSMENT

READ THE PROMPTS BELOW AND THINK ABOUT THE FIRST THING THAT COMES TO MIND. FILL YOUR ANSWERS OUT IN THE BLANK BOXES.

I AM A PERSON THAT...

LOVES	
DESIRES TO	
IS MOTIVATED BY	
IS INSPIRED BY	
HAS A HABIT OF	
IS MOST JOYOUS WHEN	
BELIEVES IN	
WOULD GIVE	
WILL ONE DAY	
HAS THE GOAL OF	
WHO REALIZES	
IS FEARFUL OF	

ROLL THE DICE
ANXIETY BREAK

Roll the dice and perform the three anxiety breaks of the number you get.
Feel free to continue these breaks daily.

	1	**2**	**3**
⚅	Take 5 deep breaths	Move the right side of your body	Move the left side of your body
⚄	Touch your right foot with your left hand 7 times	Touch your left foot with your right hand 7 times	Touch your hands overhead and try to balance on one foot
⚃	March in place with your knees high	Move the upper half of your body	Move the lower half of your body
⚂	Bring your left elbow to your right knee 7 times	Bring your right elbow to your left knee 7 times	Give yourself a big hug for 12 seconds
⚁	Jump in place 12 times	Rub your right arm with your left fist	Rub your left arm with your right fist
⚀	Squeeze your left hand with your right hand	Squeeze your right hand with your left hand	Make 7 large circles with your arms

137

GRATITUDE

/   /

TAKEAWAYS FOR THE MONTH

1 _____

2 _____

3 _____

SHARE WHAT YOU HAVE LEARNED NEW

_____

_____

_____

SHARE SOME OF THE DIFFICULTIES YOU ENCOUNTERED

_____

_____

_____

SHARE WHAT YOU'VE DONE FOR YOURSELF THIS MONTH

_____

_____

_____

HAS PRACTICING DAILY GRATITUDE HELPED WITH ANXIETY THIS MONTH?

| YES | MAYBE | NO |

SQUARE BREATHING
ANXIETY BREAK

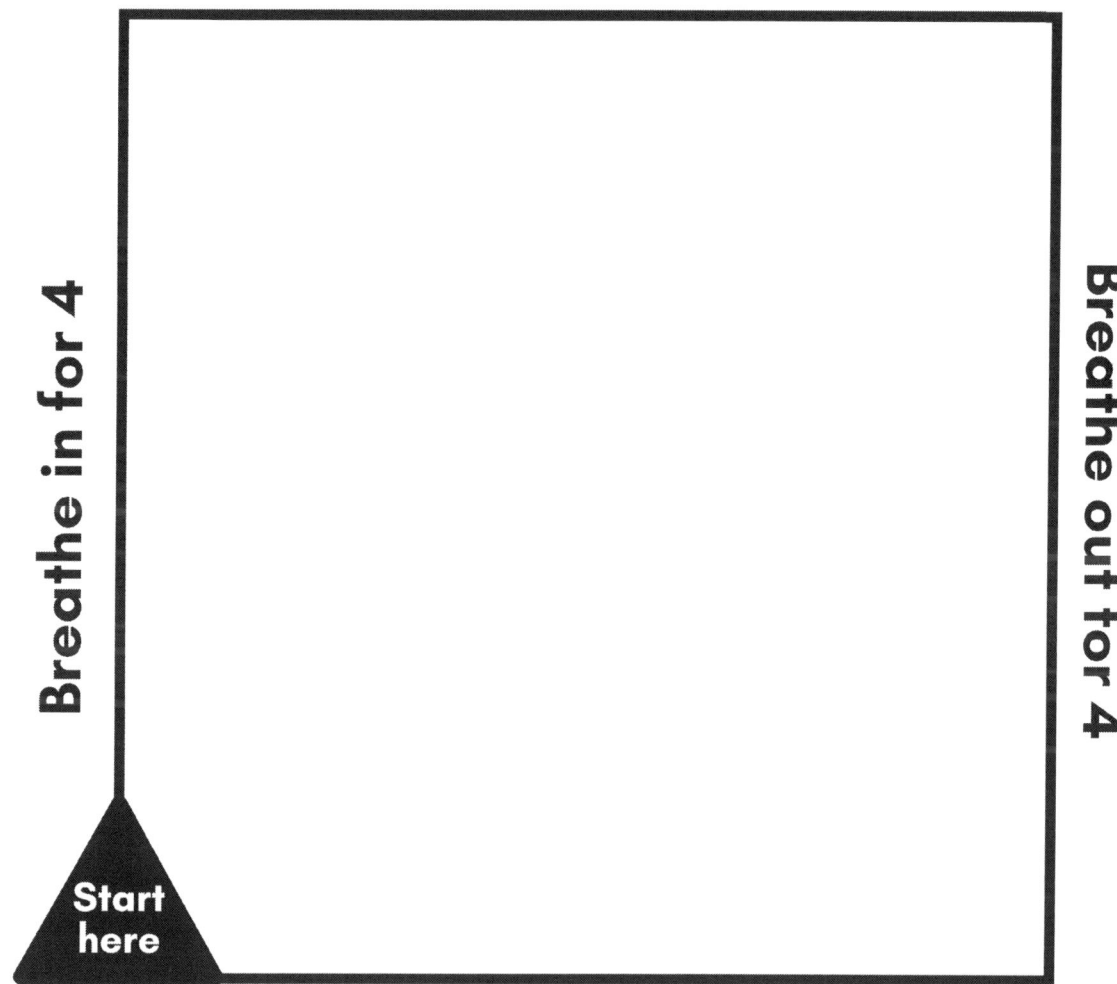

Hold for 4

Breathe in for 4

Breathe out for 4

Start here

Hold for 4

Start at the bottom left of the square. Trace your finger up the side, while you take a deep breath in. Hold your breath for four seconds as you trace the second side. Breathe out as you slide down the other side. Hold your breath for four seconds, as you trace the bottom of the square.

References

Cannon, Walter. *Bodily Changes in Pain, Hunger, Fear and Rage. New York, NY: D. Appleton & Company; 1915.*

Canva, Inc. 2022. *Images and Templates. www.canva.com. Download: 11 Sept. 2022.*

Getty Images (Celiosk), 2022. Wellness Cover Photo. Canva, Inc. www.canva.com. Downloaded 28 Sept 2022.

Shutterstock*, Inc. (2022, August). Fight or Flight Response Illustration.* https://www.shutterstock.com/image-vector/fight-flight-response-vector-illustration-labeled-1335579527

Spitzer RL, Kroenke K, Williams JB, Lowe B. *A brief measure for assessing generalized anxiety disorder: the GAD-7. Archives of internal medicine.* May 22 2006;166(10):1092-1097. PMID: 16717171

Tindle J, Tadi P. *Neuroanatomy, Parasympathetic Nervous System.* [Updated 2020 Nov 15]. In: StatPearls [Internet]. Treasure Island (FL): StatPearls Publishing; 2021 Jan-. Available from: https://www.ncbi.nlm.nih.gov/books/NBK553141/

Unknown. (2021, September). *Walter Cannon: Stress and Fight or Flight Theories.* https://study.com/academy/lesson/walter-cannon-stress-fight-or-flight-theories.html.

Walker, P. (2003). The 4Fs: A Trauma Typology in Complex PTSD. Pete-Walker.com. *http://pete-walker.com/fourFs_TraumaTypologyComplexPTSD.htm*

Bookings

To book Chanell for:

Speaking Engagements
Panel Appearances
Interviews
Trainings

Please contact her at:

CF@chanellfinley.com
www.chanellfinley.com

Made in the USA
Middletown, DE
10 April 2025

74064082R00086